# Seasons of Grief
## and Healing

James E. Miller

Augsburg
MINNEAPOLIS

## SEASONS OF GRIEF AND HEALING

Cover photo by James E. Miller
Cover design by Nicole Sletten
Book design by Michelle L. Norstad

Originally published as *Winter Grief, Summer Grace: Returning to Life After a Loved One Dies* © 1995 by James E. Miller.

"Winter" from *Chills and Fever* by John Crowe Ransom, © 1924 by Alfred A. Knopf, Inc., and renewed in 1952 by John Crowe Ransom is reprinted by permission of the publisher.

ISBN 0-8066-4036-7

Manufactured in the U.S.A.

AF 9-4036

04     03     02     01     00     1     2     3     4     5     6     7     8     9     10

*To Bernie, life of my life.*

*O Lord, go with each of us to rest;*
*if any awake, temper to them*
*the dark hours of watching;*
*and when the day returns, return to us,*
*our Sun and Comforter,*
*and call us with morning faces*
*. . . eager to labor, eager to be happy*
*. . . and if the day be marked for sorrow,*
*strong to endure it.*
—Robert Louis Stevenson
(Written and read to his family the night before his sudden death)

# Foreword

The death of someone you love is disturbing and frightening. It may be one of the most painful, anxiety-producing experiences you have ever known. You may wonder how you can survive the enormous emptiness and grief you feel.

I have written this book for you. I have attempted to help you understand how natural the grieving process is—how natural your feelings are, how natural are the various changes and directions your grieving may take—in short, how natural *you* are.

A few generations ago, a book like this would have been unnecessary—unthinkable, in fact. People knew about grieving because it was a natural part of life. It was both understandable and understood. People of all ages lived with it and honored it. But ours is a different time. And because so many of us are ill-informed about and ill at ease with dying and death and grief, your task is even more difficult.

I hope you will read these pages slowly and meditatively. Allow the words to speak to you. Let the pieces of wisdom from throughout the ages comfort and enlighten you. Spend some quiet time with the activity suggestions as ways to usher yourself through this significant and delicate time in your life.

Whatever you do with this book, I hope you will remember its basic message and promise: grief is both natural and necessary and, in your grieving, you are not alone. There is Someone who has promised to walk with you through your grief—to comfort, sustain, and strengthen you. Draw on God's promise and power as you struggle through your pain. Grieve and you will feel better in time. Mourn and you will be healed.

*Jim Miller*

James E. Miller
Fort Wayne, Indiana

*S*omeone who gave your life meaning has died.
Someone who brought you joy,
someone who gave you love,
perhaps even someone who gave you life, is gone.
No matter how much you may have prepared yourself,
you were not quite prepared.
No matter how many words you may have shared,
there were things you did not get to say.
No matter how much pain you may have endured already,
you are being called upon to endure still more.
Someone who has been a part of your days on earth
no longer walks the earth with you.
Life is not the same.
And it hurts.

*W*hen your relationship first began,
you did not think about how it would end.
You did not think about what to do when this happened,
or where you would turn,
or how you would feel.
You did not imagine you would ache in all the ways you do.
You didn't know how unpredictable your feelings would be,
how easily your mind would wander,
how quickly your energy would vanish.
You didn't think what would happen to your daily routines,
or what would become of your nightly rituals,
or how those around you would respond.
You did not know.
You *could* not know.
And now you are learning.

*T*here are many ideas about a time of loss.
There are different theories about forms grief will take,
    and the order in which it will take them.
There may be suggestions about "the right way" to grieve.
You may come to wonder what the right way really is.
Fortunately, there is an answer.
The right way is *your* way.
No one else in the world, no matter how close they are,
    has had your relationship with the person who died.
No one else has your temperament,
    or your unique ways of dealing with stress,
        or your previous experiences with losses.
No one else is you.
So the best way to move through this time of grief
    is your own way.

*R*emember: grief can be good for you.
Grieving is a natural way of helping you come to accept
    that someone you love is gone and will not return.
Grieving is a natural way to let go of life as you once knew it,
    so you can hold on to what will never leave you
        and what you will always know.
Grieving is as natural as nature itself:
    as natural as summer being cropped by autumn,
        and autumn slipping away into winter,
            and winter awakening into spring,
                and spring blossoming into summer again.
But grieving is more than nature's way.
It is the way of nature's Grand Designer,
    the One behind all that is and all that shall be,
        the One who upholds you and all those you love,
            including that person who is gone but with you still.

# *Autumn*

*The long sobs*
*Of the violins*
*Of Autumn*
*Pierce my heart.*
   —PAUL VERLAINE

*The presence of that absence is everywhere.*
      —Edna St. Vincent Millay


*Thou dost hold my eyelids from closing;*
*I am so troubled that I cannot speak.*
*I consider the days of old,*
*I remember the years long ago.*
*I commune with my heart in the night;*
*I meditate and search my spirit:*
*"Will the Lord spurn for ever,*
*and never again be favorable?"*
      —Psalm 77:4-7


*Autumn*

*There is a sob to autumn, and it is the sob of loss.*

What was once living, dies.
What was once vibrant, withers.
What was once abundant, fades away.
What remains behind is diminished.
You have known the intrusion of an autumn in your life, too,
    and you have experienced the sense of emptiness it brings.
You may have been shocked by your loved one's death,
    so shocked you became numb, confused, disoriented.
You may have disbelieved the one who died was really gone.
You may find it hard to believe even now.
Sometimes the only way to feel is to try not to feel.
Sometimes the only way to grasp what has happened
    is to hold it at a distance until you can grasp its truth,
        little by little,
            piece by piece.

*I* am weary with my moaning;
*every night I flood my bed with tears;*
*I drench my couch with my weeping.*
*My eye wastes away because of grief.*
        —Psalm 6:6-7

*Y* ou are healed of a suffering
*only by experiencing it to the full.*
        —Marcel Proust

*Autumn*

*Y*ou may be sadder than you thought possible.
   You may be filled with fear
        for what is happening now,
           for what is yet to come.
You may be afraid without even knowing what you fear.
You may become unexpectedly angry
   for no good reason or for every reason in the world.
You may be irritated with people who don't understand you,
   angry with the one who has left you,
      infuriated at what you feel God has done to you.
You may feel guilty about things you did or wish you'd done,
   about things you felt or wish you'd felt.
You may feel anxious, without knowing why.
You may feel constantly weary or completely exhausted.
You may feel lonely even when others are around,
   or *especially* when others are around.

*T*o weep is to make less the depth of grief.
—William Shakespeare

*S*eeing is believing,
but feeling is God's own truth.
—Irish Proverb

*Autumn*

*Y*ou may be on a roller coaster of emotions.
 One moment you feel steady and balanced,
  the next moment you're dissolving into tears.
One moment you possess a quiet sense of peace,
 and the next, you're feeling desperately alone.
Like many people, you may wonder if you're a little crazy.
That's a common reaction, and even to be expected;
 this is a crazy time in your life,
  when it makes sense to be a little out of your senses.
More than anything, this is a time to feel whatever you feel
 and to feel it as fully as you are able.
Remember that your feelings are neither good nor bad—
 they are simply yours to be experienced, to be honored.
The more you can accept your feelings for what they are,
 and the more you can express them in your own way,
  the better off you'll be, both today and tomorrow.

*As the rain hides the stars,*
*as the autumn mist hides the hills,*
*as the clouds veil the blue of the sky,*
*so the dark happenings of my lot*
*hide the shining of Thy face from me.*
*Yet, if I may hold Thy hand in the darkness, it is enough.*
*For I know that, though I may stumble in my going,*
*Thou dost not fall.*
  —Gaelic Prayer


*You need not cry very loud;*
*God is nearer to us than we think.*
  —Brother Lawrence


*Autumn*

*Y*ou are learning what others learned before you:
    grief is hard work.
It saps your body and mind, your heart and soul.
Yet you are doing precisely what you need to do,
    because the only cure for grief is to grieve.
The only way *beyond* this experience
    is *through* this experience.
Your only path to healing leads directly through your hurting.
It is a path you would rather not take,
    but one you must take.
It is a path that others have taken before you, many others.
They have prepared the way for you.
Their spirits accompany you.
So does the greatest Spirit of all,
    the One who will not leave you comfortless,
        no matter where you go, no matter what you do.
However alone you may feel, you are never truly alone.

# $S$uggestions

### Seek out a listener.
Most grieving people find that it helps to share their thoughts and feelings with another person. There are caring people who will welcome the role of listener. You may turn naturally to a best friend or close family member. You may seek out a neighbor or colleague who has lost a loved one in the past. You may choose to speak to a clergy person, a grief counselor, or other professional. Whatever you do, talk with someone.

### Select a "phone friend."
If you feel extremely sad or depressed—especially at night—ask someone to be your telephone partner—someone who will expect you to call when you feel low, day or night. Just knowing there's someone to call is often a help in itself. Keep their phone number where it's easy to find, and do call when you need to.

### Link yourself with the one who died.
If it feels comforting, do something physical to connect yourself to the one you have loved. Place their picture in your purse or wallet or inside a locket. Wear a piece of their jewelry or carry a favorite possession of theirs in your pocket. Drink from their mug or write with their pen. Find your own way to be close to them.

*Preserve keepsake memorials.*
Your loved one's life was significant—and so was their death, so save mementos of this time if you wish. Clip the obituary from the newspaper or save the entire newspaper in which it appeared. Keep the funeral bulletin. You might request a copy of the sermon or the entire funeral service. Cards and notes from friends and family may mean even more at a later time.

*Keep a journal during this time.*
Write whatever you want, as often as you want. Keep a notebook for just this purpose. Date each entry in case you decide to go back over your words one day. Don't censor yourself; write freely and naturally. Include your feelings. Some people like to write letters to the one who died; others write to God.

*Delve into something inspirational.*
Dip regularly into resources that feed your spirit—devotional writings, prayers or meditations, sermons, poetry, hymns. Spend time with the Bible—perhaps the book of Psalms will hold special meaning during this time. Or try stories from the New Testament Gospels or Paul's letters to the Corinthians. Borrow, rent, or purchase audio and videotapes, or compact disks that suit your needs

# *Winter*

Two evils, monstrous either one apart,
Possessed me, and were long and
    loath at going:
A cry of Absence, Absence,
    in the heart,
And in the wood the
    furious winter blowing.
                    —JOHN CROWE RANSOME

*Lord of the universe,*
*I do not beg You to reveal to me the secret of Your ways,*
*for who am I to know them?*
*But show me one thing,*
*show it to me more clearly and more deeply,*
*show me what this which is happening at this very moment*
*means to me,*
*what it demands of me,*
*what You, Lord of the world,*
*are telling me by way of it.*
*Dear God, I do not ask You to take away my suffering;*
*I don't even want to know why I suffer;*
*but only this, my God—*
*do I suffer for Your sake?*
　　　—Levi Yitzhak of Beditchev

*Winter*

*W**inter can be the cruelest season of the year,*
cold and dreary, depressing and long.
This can also be true of your grief's winter:
the air feels raw, days grow tedious, nights go on forever.
The numbness that first shielded you has worn away.
Now you must face head-on what lies all around you:
all that you miss and all that you fear,
all your sorrow and all your dread.
There can be a piercing loneliness to winter grief.
Not only are you separated from the one who died,
but you can also feel isolated from those around you,
perhaps even alienated from yourself.
People who do not understand how plodding grief can be
may not be ready to bear all your moods or moans.
And your world can appear so different,
so silent, so stark, so empty.
This is exactly the world you need.

*We are not forced to take wings to find Him,*
*but have only to seek solitude*
*and to look within ourselves.*
      —Teresa of Avila


*They who wait for the Lord shall renew*
      *their strength,*
*they shall mount up with wings*
      *like eagles,*
*they shall run and not be weary,*
*they shall walk and not faint.*
      —Isaiah 40:31


*Winter*

*T*he winter of your grief is a time to do what is best for you:
a time to *be*, just to be.
A part of you may wish to push ahead.
Winter says, "Take your time."
A part of you may wish to get this over with quickly.
Winter says, "Be patient."
Something within you may want to escape.
Winter says, "This is what you need right now."
This is a chance to do what you may not often do:
sit and be quiet,
walk and be aware,
write or talk and be reflective.
You can spend time with yourself and make a close, close friend.
You can immerse yourself in the stillness and let it inform you.
You can open your eyes to the starkness that is around you
and find unusual beauty.
You can use this time of barrenness to begin your healing.

*Be strong and of good courage;*
*be not frightened, neither be dismayed:*
*for the Lord your God is with you wherever you go.*
  —Joshua 1:9

*He who lacks time to mourn,*
*lacks time to mend.*
  —William Shakespeare

*Winter*

*I*t may seem to others that not much is happening now.
You may feel that way yourself.
Yet much *is* going on, much *is* stirring underneath.
Just as fields of whiteness can hide what is underground,
     so can days of quiet mask what is shifting inside you.
As you confront reminders of your loss day by day,
     you make room for that unyielding absence,
          and prepare bit by bit for what life yet holds.
As you allow yourself to revisit other losses you have known,
     you can encourage the mending you have already begun.
As you realize that you cannot make it by yourself,
     you can reach out to those sources of strength
          —and to *that* Source of strength—
               that guided you before, that guide others now.
In what seems like a static time, you will begin moving forward.

*Fear not, for I have redeemed you;*
*I have called you by name, you are mine.*
*When you pass through the waters I will be with you;*
*and through the rivers, they shall not overwhelm you;*
*when you walk through fire you shall not be burned,*
*and the flame shall not consume you.*
*For I am the Lord your God, the Holy One of Israel, your Savior.*
    —Isaiah 43:1b–3

*Let nothing disturb you;*
*Let nothing dismay you;*
*All things pass,*
*God never changes.*
*Patience attains*
*All it strives for.*
*He who has God*
*Finds he lacks nothing.*
*God alone suffices.*
    —Teresa of Avila

*Winter*

*I*n a time when much may seem beyond your control,
　　there are things you can do, things that are worth doing.
You can be as kind to yourself as to your best friend;
　　and you deserve that, especially right now.
You can monitor any guilt you might be carrying
　　and look for ways to let go of it.
Guilt benefits no one—not you, not the people around you,
　　not the person who died.
You can spend time in nature where so much waits to greet you,
　　to assure you and renew you.
You can be among people who support and lift you,
　　and together you can learn an invaluable lesson:
　　　　grief shared is grief diminished.
You can diminish your grief by sharing it another way:
　　with a God who understands, even if you cannot know;
　　　　who holds you, even when you may not be sure;
　　　　　　who guides you, even where the way is not clear.
In the winter of your grief, God winters with you.

# $S$uggestions

**Walk out of doors, be in nature.**
Walking improves muscle tone and increases blood circulation. It releases chemicals in your brain that can even help you feel better. Being surrounded by God's created world has its own positive effects. You can find your moods reflected there. You can see examples of healing and growth all around you. Seen with the right eyes, you can be surrounded with wonder. Time spent in nature grounds you and frees you. Walk outside at least once a day if you can.

**Volunteer your time.**
Even when you're grieving, you can do things for others. If you have the energy and if you wish, volunteer for an organization whose goals you respect. This can help break up long days alone and benefit other people at the same time. There can be a grace and an appreciation for life in being among children or older people or those people who need you.

**Create a memory book.**
Put together a scrapbook depicting the life of the one who died. Gather photographs, postcards and letters, reminders of trips and special events, and other memorabilia to help tell the story. Organize the book in your own way. When you're done, share it with someone who would appreciate its significance.

*Winter*

### Consider a support group.

It's surprising how much you can learn from and help one another. No one understands what you're going through like someone who is going through something similar. Perhaps a congregation in your area has a group in place. Check with your local hospice, hospital, cancer society, or funeral home.

### Prepare for special days.

Birthdays, anniversaries, holidays, and other significant days can be especially difficult. Rather than stewing and worrying as these days approach, take an active role in planning how you will celebrate. Make a place in your day to remember your loved one—it would be unnatural not to. You can do this privately, with a close friend or relative, or with a group of people. Plan other special things for your day, perhaps things you've never done before.

### Journal.

If you haven't had the energy to write before, consider starting now. If you've been writing, keep it up. Try writing at least once a day. Make a ritual of it—pour yourself a cup of tea or coffee, sit in a favorite place, and set a picture of the one you love nearby. Then write as much as you wish. As the days pass, flip back through your previous entries and note your progress.

# Spring

And time remembered is grief forgotten
And frosts are slain and flowers begotten,
And in green underwood and cover
Blossom by blossom the spring begins.

—ALGERNON CHARLES SWINBURNE

*Grief melts away*
*Like snow in May,*
*As if there were no such cold thing.*
    —George Herbert


*Lo, the winter is past, the rain is over and gone.*
*The flowers appear on the earth,*
*the time of singing has come,*
*and the voice of the turtledove is heard in our land.*
    —Song of Solomon 2:11–12

*Spring*

*S*pring has such fragile beginnings:
  a tiny shoot of green here,
     a hint of pastel there,
        a bud that only half opens.
Sometimes spring comes so subtly you almost miss it.
But once it begins, there is no stopping it;
  as it spreads, there is no mistaking it.
The morning sun brings sounds that were not there before.
The breeze carries a warmth
  that invites you to venture outside yourself.
A promise is released with the budding and the blossoming,
  and it showers you with new hope.
What you experience in the springtime of the year
  is what you can experience in the springtime of your grief.
There comes a time of growing radiance.
And the radiance is not just around you—
  it is within you.

*Be like the bird*
*That, pausing in her flight*
*Awhile on boughs too slight,*
*Feels them give way*
*Beneath her and yet sings,*
*Knowing that she hath wings.*
   —Victor Hugo

*Everything in life that we really accept undergoes a change.*
*So Suffering must become Love.*
*This is the mystery.*
*This is what I must do.*
*I must pass from personal love to greater love.*
      —Katherine Mansfield

*Spring*

*T*his season cannot be all brightness and glow, however.
You still feel sad at times.
You get caught off-guard by sudden rushes of painful emotions.
That's the nature of spring—
    gradual warming punctuated by brief stabs of chill.
Yet as you let your feelings evolve in ways most fitting to you,
    you promote the natural unfolding of your grief,
        the natural unfolding of your life.
You can begin to direct more and more
    what is happening around you.
You can decide about those things you want to start doing again.
You can experiment with things you've never tried before,
    realizing that something within you now is eager to try.
You can begin to turn your attention more to others,
    offering what you have to give,
        welcoming what is there to receive.
You have every reason to do both,
    and every right.

*O*ften the test of courage is not to die but to live.
—Vittorio Alfieri

*G*reat grief is a divine and terrific radiance
which transfigures the wretched.
—Victor Hugo

*Spring*

*P*salm 118 in the Bible contains this line:
    *I shall not die, but I shall live.*
That's the message the spring of your grief contains:
    the discovery that, yes, you *will* live.
But it's more than a discovery—it's also a decision:
    "I shall not allow myself to die; I choose to live again."
You may trace that shift within you
    to a particular moment in time.
Perhaps it's a sense of optimism
    that awakens with you one morning.
Maybe it's hearing yourself laugh
    for the first time in a long, long time.
Perhaps it's being captured by a dream
    that leaves you feeling freer, and more at peace.
Something buds, something opens up—and it's you.
You realize your attention is being drawn to the future again.
You feel a spirit re-forming, a spirit you have missed.
You sense an energy re-gathering, one you have longed for.
Your "best self" is on its way back.

*L*ord, be thou within me, to strengthen me;
without me, to keep me;
above me, to protect me;
beneath me, to uphold me;
before me, to direct me;
behind me, to keep me from straying;
round about me, to defend me.
— Lancelot Andrewes


*W*eeping may tarry for the night,
but joy comes with the morning.
— Psalm 30:5b


*Spring*

*B*ut something more is at work.
However much *you* decide to return,
    you may also sense that a decision is being made *for* you,
        and it comes from outside you.
New life is not just a choice you make—
    it is an opportunity you are offered, a gift you are given.
It is not just something you do—it is something you accept.
It is not something you force—it is something you trust.
And in the trusting you encourage your healing.
For the God of all creation,
    the Maker of each season in nature,
        is also the Guide through each season of your grief.
What is happening to you is not mere happenstance.
Something larger than you is at work within you.
Someone wiser than you has a word to speak,
    and that word is
        *Yes.*

# Suggestions

**Invite loved ones to an evening of sharing.**
Ask a close friend or several friends or relatives over. Eat a meal that your loved one might have enjoyed. Light a candle at the table in that person's memory. After dinner, reminisce and tell one another stories. Get out some of your photos and reminders. Be ready to laugh and feel free to cry.

**Keep your loved one's name and spirit alive through an act of love.**
Donate to a cause in your loved one's memory. Or start a fund to which you and others can contribute, one that will further some goal your loved one believed in or might have supported. Or organize a volunteer project that your loved one would have been a part of, were he or she alive.

**Invest your loved one's possessions in others.**
When the time is right, distribute things you wish others to have. Certain cherished possessions will hold special meaning for close friends or family members. Clothing and other articles may benefit someone you know or someone you've never met.

**Create a living memorial.**
On special days—or even ordinary ones—plant a seed or a bulb, a bush or a tree, in honor of your special one. Tend it and watch it grow. Consider adding something more with the changing seasons or after another year. Explain to friends and family what you have done, and let them enjoy the memorial too.

*Spring*

*Expand your horizons.*
Do something you've often wanted to do but have never taken the time to do. Undertake a new hobby. Learn a new skill. Travel somewhere you've dreamed of going, or return to a place you've been before—but this time do it on your own. Enroll in a class. Join a social group. Make some new friends.

*Change something visible to express the changes within you.*
As you become aware that you're not the same person you used to be, and that your life is not quite the same, mark that change in some tangible way. If it feels right, do something different with your personal appearance or your wardrobe. You might redecorate some part of your home or turn a room over to a whole different purpose.

*Watch for other people who are newly bereaved.*
When you feel ready, offer something of yourself to persons who are beginning the journey that you began a while ago. You will be able to understand them and to speak to them in a way that many others cannot. Offer your compassion. Give silent witness to the hope and assurance you are discovering.

# *Summer*

In the midst of winter
I found at last
there was within myself
an invincible summer.
—ALBERT CAMUS

*W*hat we once enjoyed and deeply loved we can never lose,
for all that we love deeply becomes part of us.
  —Helen Keller

*T*he worst is done and it has been mended,
and all will be well,
and all will be well,
and all manner of things will be well.
  —Julian of Norwich

*Summer*

*S*pring leads ever so naturally into summer.
   New shades of green appear.
Leaves grow full and varied,
   plants reach upward and outward,
      fields blanket themselves in bold displays of color.
The sun stays longer than before.
Mornings begin brighter,
   afternoons turn warmer,
      evenings beckon as they have not in a long while.
There is a sense of renewed vitality.
What happens around you in nature
   can also happen within you in your grief.
Something begins to take root and hold.
Something quickens with life.
But this is more than just something within you.
It *is* you.

*One who has journeyed in a strange land
cannot return unchanged.*
 —C. S. Lewis

*To yield is to be preserved whole.
To be bent is to become straight.
To be empty is to be full.
To be worn out is to be renewed.*
 —Lao Tsu

*Summer*

This new life blossoming within you
    grows out of all you have undergone,
        all you have done.
This summertime of your grief does not just arrive on its own;
    you invite it to come.
You summon it by making your way through all your pain,
    so that you can welcome what lies on the far side of pain:
        the possibility of thanksgiving and joy and hope.
You encourage this experience of summer
    as you face your fears and doubts,
        the silence and the aloneness.
Because then you can greet what is taking hold within you:
    fortitude and faith, inner strength and outer awareness.
This new life of yours also has another source, a larger one.
For while you invited this change, you did not create it.
While you nurtured it, you are not responsible for its birth.
It comes to you as a gift.
A grace.

*You* have delivered my soul from death,
my eyes from tears, my feet from stumbling.
I walk before the Lord in the land of the living.
  —Psalm 116:8–9 (NRSV)

*A* deep distress has humanized my soul.
  —William Wordsworth

*Summer*

*S*ummer grace flows directly from winter grief.
It presents itself in paradoxes.
However hard it is for you to let go,
 once you have, something surprising happens: you grasp.
You grasp a new depth of feeling
 for what others must go through.
You grasp wisdom about what life offers, and how it offers it.
You grasp appreciation for all you've been given.
However painful it is for you to accept the reality of death,
 once you have done so, something else happens:
  you become more truly alive.
You become more ready to treasure this miracle called life.
You become more prepared for other experiences of rebirth.
You become more open to thoughts of your own death,
 as you come to realize all that death cannot take away,
  all that death cannot destroy.
You come to know that within every ending lies a beginning.

*Your sun shall no more go down,*
*nor your moon withdraw itself;*
*for the Lord will be your everlasting light,*
*and your days of mourning shall be ended.*
  —Isaiah 60:20

*Life is real! Life is earnest!*
*And the grave is not its goal;*
*Dust thou art, to dust returnest,*
*Was not spoken of the soul.*
  —Henry Wadsworth Longfellow

*Summer*

However painful it is to bid farewell to one who has died,
once you have done so,
you begin a new relationship with them,
one you can always cherish.
Once you release them from earthly time,
you can embrace them in eternity.
When you release them from the physical dimension,
you can hold them close in a dimension no less real:
the spiritual one.
For, even though they no longer walk beside you,
they will be even closer.
They will be *within* you.
And you will not forget them, because you *cannot* forget them.
They will be as near to you as your own breathing,
and as much a part of you as your own dreaming.
They will exist in you as love.

*If we live, we live to the Lord,*
*and if we die, we die to the Lord;*
*so then, whether we live or whether we die,*
*we are the Lord's.*
—Romans 14:8

*Deep, unspeakable suffering*
*may well be called a baptism,*
*a regeneration, the initiation*
*into a new state.*
—George Eliot

*A*s you journey through your seasons of grief,
you discover what countless others discovered before:
that you have changed.
You will never again be the person you once were.
You will have lost,
but in addition to the losing—*because* of the losing—
you will have gained.
You will be yourself, and you will be more than yourself.
Some people describe this process as transformation.
Others call it resurrection.
Whatever words you choose,
the result is the same.
Something new will have happened.
Something original will have come to life.
Something unexpected will have been born.

*I* am like a child who awakes
At the light, so safe and so sure.
Free from night's fears when dawn breaks,
In Thee I am ever secure.
    —Rainer Maria Rilke
        (translated by Jessie Lemont)


*T* hou that has given so much to me,
Give one thing more—
    a grateful heart,
Not thankful when it pleases me,
As if thy blessings had spare days;
But such a heart
Whose very pulse may be
Thy praise.
        —George Herbert

*T*he writer of the book of Isaiah offered a promise long ago
that people in the winter of grief have held onto.
If ever there were words of summer grace, these are they:

> *For you shall go out in joy, and be led forth in peace;*
> *the mountains and the hills before you*
>     *shall burst forth into singing,*
> *and all the trees of the field shall clap their hands.*

This is the experience that awaits you.
You shall know joy once more,
    and you shall rest again in peace.
For God who makes mountains and hills burst into song,
    the One who makes trees of the field clap their hands,
        is the same One who can make
            this paradox of life in death a reality.
As you experience that reality in your life,
    as you look back upon the seasons you have known,
        you may be able to make this affirmation:

*I* have known the blessing of sharing time with another,
    one whom I have loved deeply.
I have been enriched by their life,
    and I have felt diminished by their death.
I have lived it all:
        the laughter and the tears,
            the singing and the sighing,
                the darkness and the light.
I have known how the world can change before your eyes
    when you lose the one you love so much.
I have felt lonely and alone.
Like so many others,
    I have been acquainted with grief.
Like so many others,
    I have been taught the mysterious lessons of mourning.

*I* have learned that as I let go, something will always remain,
   that as I bid farewell, someone will always abide.
I have learned that love does not end—not even with death;
   it continues to express itself in ways ever new.
When I am most alone, the Spirit of God accompanies me,
   when I am most afraid, the Promise of God comforts me,
      when I am most fragile, the Hand of God upholds me.
I see that, however much I did not wish for this loss,
   my time of losing can also be a time of gaining.
For I can come to appreciate life as I never have before.
I can experience and cherish growth as I would not otherwise do.
I can share in ways that might not otherwise be possible.
I am learning to see the ways in which I have been blessed
   by the God who walked with me through grief of winter,
      who accompanies me into the grace of summer's new life.

*O* *Thou full of compassion,*
   *I commit and commend myself unto Thee,*
   *in whom I am, and live, and know.*
*Be Thou the Goal of my pilgrimage, and my Rest by the way.*
*Let my soul take refuge from the crowding turmoil*
   *of worldly thoughts beneath the shadow of Thy wings;*
*let my heart, this sea of restless waves,*
   *find peace in Thee, O God.*
                    —St. Augustine

*Acknowledgments*

I am indebted to many people who shared the stories of their losses with me, teaching me so much. Various colleagues have been instrumental in shaping my thinking about grief and mourning: John Schneider, Ken Doka, Donna O'Toole, John Peterson, Jennifer Levine, Dick Gilbert, Paul Johnson, and Patrick Del Zoppo. My writing has been improved by Bernie Miller and Clare Barton looking over my shoulder, but especially by the sensitive and judicious work of my editor, Bob Klausmeier.